Charlotte Zolotow

flocks of birds

Illustrated by
Ruth Lercher Bornstein

Thomas Y. Crowell   New York

Flocks of Birds
Text copyright © 1965 by Charlotte Zolotow
Illustrations copyright © 1981 by Ruth Lercher Bornstein
The text of *Flocks of Birds* was originally published by
Abelard-Schuman in 1965. All rights reserved. Printed in
the United States of America. No part of this book may
be used or reproduced in any manner whatsoever without
written permission except in the case of brief quotations
embodied in critical articles and reviews. For information
address Thomas Y. Crowell Junior Books, 10 East 53rd Street,
New York, N.Y. 10022. Published simultaneously in
Canada by Fitzhenry & Whiteside Limited, Toronto.

Typography by Kohar Alexanian

Library of Congress Cataloging in Publication Data

Zolotow, Charlotte, 1915–
    Flocks of Birds.
    Summary: A mother soothes her youngster to sleep
with the images of a flock of birds in flight across
mountains, over lakes, and by wind-swept cities.
    [1. Birds — Fiction]   I. Bornstein, Ruth.   II. Title.
PZ7.Z77Fl   1981   [E]   81-43029
ISBN 0-690-04112-8   AACR2
ISBN 0-690-04113-6 (lib. bdg.)

1   2   3   4   5   6   7   8   9   10

First Edition

For Ned Shank

The little girl was already in bed
and her mother had kissed her good night.

"But I'm not sleepy," the little girl said.
"Lie here in the dark," said her mother,
"and think your thoughts until you are."

"Give me something good to think about,"
the little girl said, holding her mother's hand.
"Think of flocks of birds," her mother said.
"Close your eyes and think of flocks of birds
flying south."

"What shall I think about them?"
the little girl asked.

"Oh," said her mother, "think of a
dark meadow
in the mountains far away.
The long black grass is filled with
sleeping birds.

Think of the early morning light beginning,
and as the mist rises from the marsh,
the birds begin to stir.
By ones, by twos, by threes, the birds rise up
circling above the meadow and the marsh.

There is only one cry from one bird
as they begin their flight across the mountain,
over the valleys, over the ocean far below.
Think of the sun which suddenly comes
through the clouds like a pale orange ball.

The birds fly over the water, over the silvery sand,
over the city where people are hurrying
through the autumn wind on their
way to work.

They fly on, over towns where the littlest children
swinging on swings in the early morning
tilt their heads backward
and see the birds high above them in the sky.

Through the morning, through the afternoon,
they fly over country fields bright with goldenrod,
over farms nestling in the browning hills.

Now a school bus empties out the children
on a dusty lane and high above
the birds are flying, flying.

They fly over mountains where the trees
are yellow and crimson and brown,
and only the pines are green.

They pass over rivers where the boats cut
choppy little white-edged waves into
the windy water.
And as the long afternoon light begins
to lengthen, they fly across a hazy white
shape that is the late afternoon moon.

They fly through the long purple and
pink clouds of the sunset and through
the gathering blackness of the night.

In the town far below them, lights go on
like little stars in kitchen and living room
windows. No one hears the sound of the
birds passing high above the dark sky.

They fly across the huge harvest moon,
and over lakes where the water is like
a pool of black ink holding the moon's reflection,

and two deer stand side by side, drinking
at the water's edge.

And the birds fly on and on over another
small town where the houses are dark and
little girls like you are sleeping,
dreaming of lovely things

like flocks of birds
flying through the night
in the fall."